Who Can

Children

Driver

A Play by Joy Cowley
Illustrations by Graeme Kyle

Driver:

Who can see the camel walking by the bus?

Children:
We can see the camel,
and it can see us.

3

Driver:

Who can see the zebra running by the bus?

Children:
We can see the zebra,
and it can see us.

Driver:
Who can see the elephant
washing by the bus?

Children:
We can see the elephant,
and it can see us.

Children:
It is washing us.
Slosh! Slosh!